The Perils of Bipolarity:

Subnational Conflict and the Rise of China

Lt Col Mark O. Yeisley, USAF

Intrastate conflicts, ranging from localized rebellions to civil war, increased linearly from 1946 through 1992 and then dramatically decreased in the post-Cold War era. This rise and fall of subnational conflict closely mirrors the "proxy" wars fought by or between the Union of Soviet Socialist Republics (USSR) and the United States. Proxy refers to "(g)reat power hostility expressed through client states" and describes superpower use of these states to pursue strategic and ideological goals within the confines of nuclear deterrent postures extant during the Cold War.[1] This was done in large part to achieve strategic national interests and other political goals without risking nuclear war. In its waning years, the USSR could no longer afford to fund these wars; America ended support to many of these commitments soon after the Cold War ended.[2] With resources dried up, former client states and subgroups had little choice but to resolve these conflicts, either via negotiation or decisive victory.

The United States emerged from the Cold War as the sole superpower in a unipolar international system. However, evidence suggests this unipolarity could soon change as a new bipolar system emerges with China as the next challenger superpower. Scholars debate the likelihood of future war with a rising China, with each side arguing whether direct conflict is inevitable. Yet this debate does not consider what I suggest is the most probable future of United States–China relations; while direct conflict with China is indeed a possibility, it remains remote. I offer a quite different theory, in which subnational conflict will rise once more as the United States engages in proxy conflicts with China over resource access in Africa. These conflicts will place great demands on all US instruments of power, as involvement in counterinsurgency operations in Africa trends upward. Bipolarity and renewed proxy conflict will require rethinking of long-term national and military strategies focused primarily on large-scale interstate wars; this will impact defense acquisition and military doctrine as US strategic focus shifts from conventional conflict to counterinsurgency operations.

This paper defines subnational and proxy conflicts and explains why nuclear powers in a bipolar system make strategic policy choices to compete by proxy over contentious issues. It reviews the historical record of subnational proxy conflict conducted by the United States and the USSR from 1946 through the end of the Cold War era. This paper will discuss the rationale for my claim that China will soon be poised to challenge the United States within a new bipolar order, with a concomitant increase of proxy conflicts between the two. It reviews the implications for US grand and military strategies, as well as for defense acquisition programs and development of future doctrine to meet this new order. It concludes by discussing recommendations for strategic planning over the next several decades.

Renewed Bipolarity, Subnational Conflict and Proxy Conflicts

The modern international system in which states compete for survival has historically assumed three primary configurations: (1) unipolarity, in which a single state acts as a hegemon;[3] (2) bipolarity, in which two states control the majority of power with weaker states aligning with one or the other; and (3) multipolarity, where three or more nations are powerful enough to act as poles in the system.

Since the 1648 Treaties of Westphalia, multipolarity has been the norm, in which great power states jockeyed for power on the European continent. While the fortunes of these powers have waxed and waned, war has typically been the ultimate result of perceived power imbalances among them. While there have been historical instances of bipolarity, each of these was regional rather than global in scope.[4] When the United States and the USSR emerged from World War II as the two sole remaining great powers, the international system assumed a bipolar status for the first time and remained so until 1991, when the USSR disintegrated.[5]

Many scholars have argued that the international system has assumed a unipolar orientation, with the United States the sole remaining "superpower."[6] Of perhaps more importance are the predictions of what will follow for international relations; for example, some believe the United States will face no viable challengers in the near term, with unipolarity a stable and long term likelihood.[7] Others see a return to a multipolar environment wherein many nations will possess military and economic might sufficient to be recognized as great power states.[8] Still others foresee a return to bipolarity, with the United States and one future great power locked once again in a struggle for primacy.[9] It is this last possibility that I address in this paper. While the international system is increasingly influenced by Brazil, Russia, India, and China, I argue that China is the most likely challenger to US hegemony to emerge, at least in the foreseeable future. Only China will possess sufficient economic might to leverage into military spending and growth to rival the United States; it will soon become the second great power state in a new bipolar international regime.

Scholars have lauded bipolarity for the stability inherent in such a regime; however, these arguments focus on Cold War relations between states and reduced incidence of interstate war.[10] Indeed, the Cold War bipolar era was arguably more peaceful than the era preceding it, as major wars between states were relatively rare and no militarized conflict ever erupted between the two superpowers. Yet the incidence of violent subnational conflict increased during the same period, peaking in 1992 and falling rapidly in the nearly two decades after.[11] Was Cold War interstate stability truly an artifact of a bipolar system, or were additional factors responsible? What can explain the concurrent rise in subnational conflict observed during the same temporal period?

Bipolarity did not stifle interstate conflict between seventeenth century Britain and France when they were imperial superpowers, yet no Cold War militarized conflict broke out between the United States and the USSR.[12] The reason lies in the unique conditions of Cold War bipolarity; each superpower possessed sufficient nuclear capability to make war too costly to consider. Some scholars place this absence of conflict on the success of US deterrence and containment strategies, such as were recommended in Kennan's "Long Telegram" and subsequently employed in the Truman through Reagan administrations.[13] Others cite the "stability-instability paradox," wherein nuclear parity precludes the use of such weapons while still allowing limited conventional conflicts between nuclear-armed states.[14] Others infer that nuclear weapons played no part in Cold War peace at all.[15] I argue instead that the perceived high costs of war in nuclear parity within a bipolar international system prevented war between the two. The United States and the USSR chose instead to address ideological differences indirectly by proxy within client states. While these strategies arguably kept the Cold War cold, what prescriptive logic was responsible for these superpower decisions to engage in subnational conflict by proxy?

Subnational Conflicts

Just as interstate conflict takes many forms, from sanctions to militarized action, so too does subnational conflict cover a wide variety of cases. Civil wars often begin as grass roots organizing, followed by riots, rebellions, and insurgent conflict prior to culminating in open war between insurgent groups and forces of the state. For the purposes of this paper I use conflicts occurring solely within the geopolitical borders of the state, though examples of those spanning state borders also exist.[16] Thousands of interstate conflicts have occurred since the Treaties of Westphalia, yet they have become relatively rare in the post-WWII era. Since 1946, 61 have been recorded, but only five have been initiated since the end of the Cold War. However, the number of ongoing subnational conflicts increased steadily during that period, some lasting 50 years or more. Between 1946 and 2007 there were 225 incidences of subnational conflict between some insurgent group and the forces of the state.[17]

The number of subnational conflicts peaked in 1992 and has rapidly declined over the last two decades; ongoing conflicts in 2007 were at the same level as those observed in the 1970s.[18] This pattern of subnational conflict naturally produces two related questions: What caused the increase in ongoing subnational conflict during the Cold War, and why has it rapidly decreased in the two decades since? Both of these questions may be answered by examining the strategic foreign policy choices each superpower made during the Cold War era.

Proxy Conflicts

Proxy conflicts are those in which great power hostilities are expressed through client states rather than between great powers themselves. These proxy conflicts occur between nations that disagree over specific issues but do not wish to engage in direct conflict. A significant portion of Cold War-era subnational conflicts were proxy conflicts, supported by the United States or the USSR in support of geopolitical and ideological differences. Note that impressions of power were just as important as military equality; this resulted in strategies that depended on perceptions of a balance of power as much as the balance itself.[19] Thus US policy treated any Soviet gains as a threat that had to be countered in a zero-sum *Realpolitik* game.

Cold War proxy conflicts usually took the form of aid provided to either insurgent forces or those of the state: cash transfers, provision of weapons/technology, and advisory or combat support. While many instances of US and/or Soviet aid to states in conflict remain classified and are thus impossible to account for at present, there are still many instances where such aid was identifiable. During the Cold War dozens of subnational conflicts were proxy wars of the United States or the USSR, and their distribution is suggestive. Nearly half of these occurred during the Cold War's first two decades, when US–USSR competition was on the rise; this percentage declined in the 1980s as Soviet economic support dwindled and US aid to these nations quickly followed suit.[20] Thus while the high cost of interstate conflict in the Cold War bipolar system wherein nuclear annihilation was possible led to peace between the great powers, it increased the incidence of subnational proxy conflict via two complementary mechanisms. It provided the superpowers a means to achieve geostrategic goals without the risk of nuclear war while also providing groups within client states the means to achieve their goals, through violence if necessary.

Why did the United States and the USSR engage in Cold War proxy conflict? Realists of the period warned against doing so; involvement in Third World conflicts was detrimental to US interests and did not enhance the all-important balance of power.[21] One possible explanation is that great powers prefer to compete by proxy to achieve their strategic interests without direct conflict and engender goodwill via soft power strategies.[22] But the historical record does not support this, as great powers have often fought with one another. A more credible explanation is found in the structural conditions that existed in the Cold War international environment. As the United States and the USSR reached nuclear parity, danger of nuclear annihilation successfully deterred both sides from direct conflict. Yet each was driven to spread its ideology to the greatest extent possible, both to maximize alliance pools and achieve *Realpolitik* goals of maximum security.[23] Thus a combination of realist political goals, coupled with the reality of nuclear parity, moved each away from direct confrontation and toward goal achievement via proxy conflict in client states.

Examples of Cold War Proxy Conflicts

The earliest Cold War example of subnational proxy conflict was the Greek civil war—a communist uprising supported by Yugoslavia and

Bulgaria and countered by the Greek army, with support from the United States and the United Kingdom.[24] The United States also funded and equipped the 1954 coup in Guatemala that ousted President Guzman and ultimately led to the 36-year civil war that followed.[25] Examples in the Western Hemisphere include the Cuban revolution, the long civil war in El Salvador where the United States supported Salvadoran government forces against the left-wing Farabundo Marti National Liberation Front, as well as the funding of rebel Contras in Nicaragua.[26] Following the end of European colonization of African nations in the 1950s and 1960s, many additional cases of Cold War proxy conflict began there as well.[27]

Probably the most infamous of these was the Angolan civil war, which began in 1975 and continued until 2002; estimates of battle deaths exceed half a million. In this conflict the United States provided monetary assistance to Angolan government forces while Cuban troops participated as a Soviet expeditionary force on the side of the communist rebels.[28] Other examples include the USSR's provision of weapons to the Mengistu regime in Ethiopia, and United States/USSR backing of the civil war in Mozambique.[29] Examples in Asia include both the US-sponsored mujahedeen fighting the Soviets in Afghanistan and US involvement in the Vietnam War.[30]

Although some of these conflicts persist, many ended with the dissolution of the USSR. Support for the Nicaraguan Contras ended after the scandal broke in the United States; a negotiated peace followed two years later.[31] Moscow ended all support for the Mengistu regime in 1990; it fell to rebels soon after.[32] When backing for the Angolan conflict was withdrawn, the National Union for the Total Independence of Angola and the People's Movement for the Liberation of Angola soon agreed to a settlement.[33] Many of the conflicts during this period were arguably initiated and certainly prolonged by external support from the two superpowers; it has been argued such external support is in fact vitally necessary for successful insurgencies.[34] While neither side had direct stakes in these conflicts, desires to resolve ideological differences within the constraints of nuclear parity drove each to create national security policy that took *Realpolitik* and domestic security concerns to foreign battlefields and engage in conflict by proxy.

The rising incidence of subnational conflict during the Cold War and its decline in the current era were thus influenced by superpower policy decisions to pursue strategic goals by proxy within client states to avoid the high costs of nuclear war. As the USSR lost the ability to fund these proxy wars, it ceased such aid and the United States followed suit. Although it is impossible to prove the loss of aid was a primary causal factor in many conflict resolutions in the post-Cold War era, loss of support would likely have forced belligerents to search for alternative funding or prepare for peace. Since conflict resolutions since 1990 have occurred at nearly three times the Cold War rate, many seem to have chosen the latter.[35] The current unipolar environment appears to be more peaceful in terms of relations both between and within states. However, several states now appear capable of achieving great power status; if one of these amasses a sufficient level of economic and military might to challenge the United States, a return to international bipolarity is likely.

Future Challenges to the Current Unipolar Order

The so-called "BRIC" states—Brazil, Russia, India, and China—arguably possess the potential to rise to great power status at some future point, yet only China has both the capability and the will to do so in the near term. I offer the rationale for singling out China as the next United States peer competitor and explain how and why this competition will occur in a bipolar international regime. In addition, I outline how US–Sino competition will lead to a resurgence in subnational proxy conflict, primarily focused in Africa, as both states compete for future access to scarce strategic resources in the region.

A Modernizing China and the Return of a Bipolar System

China's economy has exploded in recent years, surpassing Japan to become the world's second largest economy (behind the United States) in the second quarter of 2010.[36] This gap is likely to decrease in the ongoing economic crisis; US growth remains sluggish while China's is again 9 percent per annum. China has embarked on an ambitious program of military modernization, acquiring advanced offensive and defensive capabilities.[37] US deficits are likely to result in reductions in defense expenditures, further decreasing the military capabilities gap.[38] China's economic and military might, coupled with a large population, point to its emergence as both a great power and a US peer competitor in the near future.

The Rise of China and Implications for Regional Control

Volumes of scholarly literature exist detailing China's rise to great power status and the likely implications thereof.[39] Given China's prodigious economic growth, it is natural to question whether such a rise will be accompanied by US–Sino conflict. I agree with other scholars that such an outcome is unlikely, primarily because of a return of nuclear parity within a bipolar environment.[40] There are, however, concerns over China's increasing need for fuel imports to support its expanding infrastructure. For example, China shows little concern with the political ideologies of regimes with which it treats; yet its willingness to deal with states like Iran and Sudan could worsen relations with the United States.[41] China's ongoing military modernization appears also designed in part to deny US ability to deter China in the near future through strategies that would focus primarily on interruptions of its oil supply through area denial or control of critical Eastern sea lines of communication.

China is expanding its web of regional alliances via arms transfers and inducements that may result in a wall of allies the United States will find difficult to penetrate in order to protect its interests in the Eastern Hemisphere.[42] China is willing to protect its interests militarily where necessary; some claim the 1996 Taiwan Crisis indicates China may be prepared to take Taiwan by force in a preemptive attack.[43] Yet evidence suggests its neighbors welcome the economic opportunities China presents to them, and believe its intentions are peaceful and focused on domestic stability and growth rather than regional dominance.[44] Since it is unlikely that any regional attempts to balance a rising China are forthcoming, at least in the near term, it falls to the United States as the peer competitor to do so. While US military preeminence is still clear, trends indicate the United States will find it increasingly difficult to compete with China over strategic resource requirements as China's geostrategic influence continues to expand.

Bipolarity, Nuclear Weapons and Sino–US Proxy Conflict in Africa

It is likely China will achieve economic and military parity with the United States in the next two decades. China currently possesses 240 nuclear warheads and 135 ballistic missiles capable of reaching the United States or its allies; it is estimated by the mid-2020s the number of nuclear warheads will double.[45] As in the Cold War, a bipolar system in which war between the United States and China is too costly will lead to policy decisions that seek conflict resolution elsewhere.[46] But why will a rising China necessarily lead to geostrategic competition with the United States, and where would this most likely occur? Unlike in the

Cold War, access to strategic resources, rather than ideology, will lie at the heart of future US–Sino competition, and the new "great game" will be played in Africa.

The Race for Access to Strategic Resources

Despite Communist Party control of the government, China is uninterested in spreading its version of communism and is much more pragmatic in its needs—securing resources to meet the needs of its citizens and improve their standard of living.[47] Some estimates show that China will overtake the United States to become the world's largest economy by 2015; rising powers usually take the necessary steps to "ensure markets, materials and transportation routes."[48]

China is the leading global consumer of aluminum, copper, lead, nickel, zinc, tin, and iron ore and its metal needs now represent more than 25 percent of the world's total.[49] In contrast, from 1970 to 1995, US consumption of all materials including metals accounted for one-third of the global total, despite representing only five percent of the global population.[50] China is the largest energy consumer, according to the International Energy Agency, surpassing the United States in its consumption of oil, coal, and natural gas in 2009.[51] As the two largest consumers of both global energy and materials, the United States and China must seek foreign policy prescriptions to fulfill future resource needs. Since the majority of these needs are nonrenewable, competition will be of necessity zero-sum, and will be conducted via all instruments of power.[52] While the United States can alleviate some of its energy needs via bio- or coal-based fuels, hydrogen, or natural gas alternatives, China lacks the technological know-how to do so and currently remains tied to a mainly nonrenewable energy resource base.

China's Strategic Focus on Africa

Africa is home to a wealth of mineral and energy resources, much of which still remains largely unexploited. Seven African states possess huge endowments of oil, and four of these possess equally substantial amounts of natural gas.[53] Africa also enjoys large endowments of bauxite (used to make aluminum), copper, lead, nickel, zinc, and iron ore, all of which are imported and highly desired by China. Recent developments in Africa serve to prove that China seeks greater access to natural resources; it has been avidly promoting Chinese development in a large number of African nations. South Africa, Africa's largest economy, has recently allowed China to help it develop its vast mineral wealth; it is China's number one African source of manganese, iron, and copper.[54] Chinese involvement in Africa is not wholly extractive; the continent provides China a booming export market for its goods and a forum to augment Chinese soft power in the region by offering alternatives to the political and economic baggage that accompanies US foreign aid.[55]

Of primary interest is open access to Africa's significant deposits of oil and other energy resources to feed its booming industrial base. For example, China has 4,000 military personnel in Sudan to protect its interests in energy and mineral investments there; it also owns 40 percent of the Greater Nile Oil Production Company.[56] It has been estimated that within the next few decades China will obtain 40 percent of its oil and gas supplies from Africa.[57] Trade and investment in Africa have also been on the rise; trade has grown more than 10 percent annually in the past decade. Between 2002 and 2004, African exports to China doubled; it now ranks third behind the United States and France in terms of total trade with the continent. Chinese investment is also growing; there are more than 700 Chinese business operations across Africa totaling over $1 billion. Aid and direct economic assistance is increasing as well, and China has forgiven the debt of some 31 African nations.[58]

The Return of Proxy Conflict to Africa

Thus, Africa is a vital foreign interest for the Chinese and must be for the United States; access to its mineral and petroleum wealth is crucial to the survival of each.[59] The nonrenewable nature of these assets means competition for them will be zero-sum. Nearly all African states have been independent entities for less than 50 years, and consolidating robust domestic institutions and stable governments remains problematic.[60] Studies show weak governments are prime targets for civil conflicts that prove costly to control.[61] Many African nations possess strategic resources and weak regimes, making them vulnerable to internal conflict as well as valuable candidates for assistance from China or the United States to help settle their domestic grievances. Access to these resources will be of vital strategic interest to each side. Competition in nuclear parity will occur by proxy via diplomatic, economic, or military assistance to one (or both) of the parties involved.

Realist claims that focusing on Third World issues is misplaced are thus fallacious; war in a future bipolar system between the United States and China remains as costly as it was during the Cold War. Because of the fragile nature of many African regimes, domestic grievances are more prone to result in conflict. US and Chinese strategic interests will dictate an intrusive foreign policy to be both prudent and vital. US–Sino proxy conflicts over control of African resources will become necessary if these great powers are to sustain their national security postures, especially in terms of strategic defense.[62] What this means for the future of US grand and military strategy, foreign policy prescriptions, future defense acquisition priorities, and military doctrine and training will now be explored.

Implications for the United States

The Obama Administration released the 2010 National Security Strategy (NSS) last year, moving away from the preceding administration's focus on preventive war and the use of the military to succeed in this effort. The new NSS instead focuses on international institutions and robust alliances to build a more peaceful world, a restructuring of the global economy, working to limit the spread of weapons of mass destruction, and combating terrorism. To do this, the

2010 NSS argues that the United States must:

> ". . . balance and integrate all elements of American power and update our national security capacity for the 21st century. We *must maintain our military's conventional superiority*, while enhancing its capacity to defeat asymmetric threats"[63] (emphasis added).

All this is based on the assumption that the current unipolar

international environment persists. If a new bipolar order arises in which

Chinese competition for scarce resources represents the new status quo,

future NSS submittals must reflect the nature of such competitive

behavior.

The current US defense budget required approximately $680

billion, more than all other nations on earth combined. To support the

current NSS, the National Military Strategy must focus on maintaining

conventional military superiority, requiring the acquisition of military

equipment that supports traditional force-on-force military operations.[64]

Yet the United States must ensure access to strategic resources as well,

and as African subnational proxy conflict rises, national and military

strategies must adapt to meet this future challenge.

While I do not suggest that the maintenance of current capability

is unnecessary, current conventional strategies focus overmuch on

fighting the last war. If the United States is to maintain access to the

strategic resources it needs to sustain its place in the future global order,

it must improve its ability to meet the asymmetric threats it will face in proxy conflicts in Africa, where counterinsurgency operations will dominate. The asymmetric nature of future conflict over African resources means defense acquisition must focus on equipping and training military and civilian counterinsurgency teams. Both military and civilian doctrine must be altered to allow robust and effective interagency actions to meet the challenges of proxy conflict that will span the continuum of counterinsurgency warfare, from information and combat operations to peace enforcement and post-conflict stability efforts.

Recommendations

Current "conventional wisdom" suggests that the United States will benefit by ending its recent forays into counterinsurgency operations, returning to conventional warfighting preparation to meet a rising China head on.[65] However, the likelihood of a direct militarized conflict between the United States and China is low, and war between the two nuclear powers is unthinkable. It is imperative that the United States reduce its focus on maintenance of conventional force superiority; it already outdistances anything that could challenge it in the near future. Instead it should better fund acquisition and training programs to deal with future asymmetric subnational warfare. Advances in interagency support to counterinsurgencies have been substantial, yet doctrinal improvements such as those covering provincial reconstruction teams and interagency cooperation for combat and Phase IV operations must continue. While US military forces have proven invaluable in the post-conflict efforts in Iraq and Afghanistan, resource constraints caused by the current financial crisis will undoubtedly force future defense cuts and require enhanced interagency involvement instead.

Reliance on conventional "business as usual" warfighting to meet the threat of a rising China will divert precious resources away from a looming crisis in US access to foreign strategic resources, especially in Africa. Tying financial aid to democratic institution building is a failed strategy; instead, the United States must employ its soft power to persuade African nations to work with us. The time to do so is now, before China's inroads into African states become insurmountable. If the United States is to secure its resource needs from Africa in the future, it must be prepared to employ all elements of hard and soft power to meet the demands of future proxy conflict on the continent.

Conclusion

The United States currently enjoys a unique position as the sole global superpower, yet it is unlikely this unipolar moment will endure much longer. China is uniquely positioned to translate rapidly expanding economic might into sufficient military resources to achieve regional hegemony and spread its influence further abroad. To meet the needs of its growing population and burgeoning economy, China must focus on obtaining strategic resources abroad. Herein lies the challenge for future US foreign policymakers. In a future bipolar system where a nuclear-equipped China and the United States require nonrenewable strategic resources, competition for such resources will be a vital strategic interest for each side.

Scholars debate whether such strategic interests will necessitate conflict between the United States and China in the future. Preparations for such conventional conflict now dominate US defense policy. I have offered an alternative future in which proxy wars with China for continued access to strategic resources in African states will be strategically justified in the future. While I do not suggest the United States drastically reduce current preparations for conventional warfighting dominance, I believe it prudent to also prepare for future proxy conflict management in Africa.

The ongoing financial crisis will undoubtedly force reductions in future defense spending if the United States is to reduce its national debt load. This will necessitate further strategic, military, and interagency doctrinal and training realignments if we are to successfully meet the challenges of future counterinsurgency operations in Africa and elsewhere. Preparations must begin soon if we are to meet the looming challenge of strategic resource competition with China. A failure to plan for this proxy competition might make a future war with China inevitable; we have only to examine Japan's reaction to its loss of strategic resource access in the early twentieth century to illuminate the consequences such a situation could easily produce.

Notes

1. Dillon Craig, "State Security Policy and Proxy Wars in Africa—Ultima Ratio Regum: Remix or Redux?" *Strategic Insights* 9, no. 1, (Spring/Summer 2010): 2. Although definitions of proxy conflict are varied, I find the one used by Craig, which he cites and expands upon, to be most useful.

2. See, for example, Alex Thomson, *An Introduction to African Politics* (New York, NY: Routledge, 2000), 160.

3. I define a unipolar system similarly to that in Christopher Layne, "The Unipolar Illusion: Why New Great Powers Will Rise," *International Security* 17, no. 4 (Spring 1993): 5 wherein a single power possesses sufficient military and economic resources to preclude any attempts to balance against it.

4. Athens and Sparta are an early example, as are Philip II's Spain and France during the sixteenth century, and Great Britain and France during the late seventeenth and early eighteenth centuries.

5. Kenneth Waltz, "The Emerging Structure of International Politics." *International Security* 18, no. 2 (Fall 1993): 44 similarly argues that this was the first case of international bipolarity in history.

6. Charles Krauthammer, "The Unipolar Moment," *Foreign Affairs* 70, no. 1 (1990); William C. Wohlforth "The Stability of a Unipolar World," *International Security* 24, no. 1 (Summer 1999): 5–41; and Michael Mastanduno "Preserving the Unipolar Moment: Realist Theories

and U.S. Grand Strategy after the Cold War," *International Security* 21, no. 4 (Spring 1997). See also Stephen Brooks and William C. Wohlforth's defense of unilateralism in "International Relations Theory and the Case against Unilateralism," *Perspectives on Politics* 3, no. 3 (2005).

7. These are made by those Christopher Layne, *The Peace of Illusions: American Grand Strategy from 1940 to the Present* (Ithaca, NY: Cornell University Press, 2006), 134–35) by what he terms "unipolar optimists," who argue that US hard power allows no likely counterbalancing because of the high costs involved.

8. One example is made in John J. Mearsheimer, *The Tragedy of Great Power Politics* (New York, NY: W. W. Norton and Company, Inc., 2001), in which he warns of the likelihood of a return of international conflict in multipolarity.

9. Layne, "The Unipolar Illusion," 5–51.

10. A detailed argument about the alleged stability of bipolar international systems can be found in Kenneth Waltz, *Theory of International Politics* (Boston, MA: McGraw Hill, 1979).

11. There were 61 interstate conflicts between 1946 and 1990, yet most of these resulted in relatively few battle deaths and were of limited duration. Uppsala Conflict Data Program (UCDP)/Peace Research Institute Oslo (PRIO), Armed Conflict Data Set, version v4–2009.

12. Other instances of regional bipolarity (e.g., Athens versus Sparta, seventeenth century Spain versus France) were also conflictual.

13. An evaluation and appraisal of the evolution of Cold War US Grand Strategy can be found in John Lewis Gaddis, *Strategies of Containment: A Critical Appraisal of American National Security Policy During the Cold War* (New York, NY: Oxford University Press, 1982).

14. Christopher Layne, *The Peace of Illusions: American Grand Strategy from 1940 to the Present* (Ithaca, NY: Cornell University Press, 2006), 176.

15. John Mueller, "The Essential Irrelevance of Nuclear Weapons: Stability in the Postwar World," *International Security* 13, no. 2 (Fall 1988): 56.

16. Jon Abbink, "Proxy Wars and Prospects for Peace in the Horn of Africa" *Journal of Contemporary African Studies* 21, no. 3 (September 2003).

17. Conflict data were obtained from the UCDP/PRIO Armed Conflict Data Set, version v4–2009, http://www.prio.no/CSCW/Datasets/Armed-Conflict/UCDP-PRIO/.

18. Ibid.

19. Gaddis, *Strategies of Containment*, 90.

20. The United States and the USSR were involved heavily in proxy conflicts in the first two decades following WWII; by the 1980s their level of involvement had dropped to less than 20 percent. Sources include John Prados, *Safe for Democracy: The Secret Wars of the CIA* (Chicago, IL: Ivan R. Dee Publisher, 2006).

21. Realists like Hans J. Morgenthau, *Politics Among Nations: The Struggle for Power and Peace* (New York, NY: Alfred A. Knopf, 1978) and Waltz, *Theory of International Politics*, have argued against US involvement in Third World proxy wars.

22. An example of nonmilitary involvement can be found in US humanitarian efforts in Haiti, yet this effort has been blasted by Venezuela and France as a US occupation attempt. Barron Youngsmith, "Proxy War: How Haiti Became a Battlefield for the Great Powers" *The New Republic*, January 30, 2010. Joseph Nye, *Soft Power: The Means to Success in World Politics* (New York, NY: PublicAffairs, 2004) also explains how soft power increases US security in the modern age.

23. Layne, *The Peace of Illusions*, 28–38.

24. Maria Nikolopoulou, *The Greek Civil War: Essays on a Conflict of Exceptionalism and Silences* (London: Ashgate Publishing, 2004). US policy for the conflict was first outlined in Pres. Harry Truman's speech of 12 March 1947, when he stated the United States should "make full use of its political, economic and, if necessary, military power in such a manner as may be found most effective to prevent Greece from falling under the domination of the USSR." John O. Iatrides, "Britain, the United States and Greece, 1945-9," in *Greek Civil War, 1943-50: Studies of Polarization,* ed. David H. Close (London: Routledge, 1993), 202.

25. Susanne Jonas, *Battle for Guatemala: Rebels, Death Squads, and U.S. Power* (Boulder, CO: Westview Press, 1991), 70. Additional

information is included in Guy Arnold, *Wars in the Third World since 1945* (London: Cassell Villiers House, 1995), 601.

26. Elisabeth Jean Wood, *Insurgent Collective Action and Civil War* (New York, NY: Cambridge University Press, 2003), 28. Corroborating information was obtained on US intentions from a speech by former secretary of state Alexander Haig to NATO on 18 February 1981, in which he states: "We consider what is happening is part of the global Communist campaign . . . to support the Marxists in El Salvador." From Martin E. Gettleman, ed., *El Salvador: Central America in the New Cold War.* (New York, NY: Grove Press, 1981). Also see Guy Arnold, *Wars in the Third World since 1945* (London: Cassell Villiers House, 1995), 594–99 and 616–20. For the Nicaraguan civil war, see Roger Miranda and William Ratliff, *The Civil War in Nicaragua: Inside the Sandinistas* (New Brunswick, NJ: Transaction Publishers, 1993).

27. Thomson, *An Introduction to African Politics*, 152–53, describes the evolution of Soviet support in Africa in its goal of expanding socialism on the continent.

28. William Minter *Apartheid's Contras: An Inquiry into the Roots of War in Angola and Mozambique* (London: Zed Books, 1994) and Arnold, *Wars in the Third World*, 362–64.

29. Richard J. Bloomfield, ed., *Regional Conflict and U.S. Policy: Angola and Mozambique* (Algonac, MI: Reference Publications, Inc., 1988) and Arnold, *Wars in the Third World*, 400–11.

30. This is not to say proxy conflict was not present in the Middle East–US cash grants to Israel. CIA support to the Afghan mujahedeen and the ouster of Mossadegh in Iran all supported US policies meant to disadvantage Western competition and forge a strategic alliance against the USSR, according to Beverley Milton-Edwards and Peter Hinchcliffe, *Conflict in the Middle East since 1945* (London: Routledge, 2001).

31. John R. Thackrah, *Routledge Companion to Military Conflict since 1945* (New York, NY: Routledge, 2009), 32.

32. Ibid., 74.

33. Raymond W. Copson, *Africa's Wars and Prospects for Peace* (Armonk, NY: M. E. Sharpe, Inc., 1994), 114–25. Although Soviet support was high through 1988, by 1990 the USSR no longer had the will to fund the conflict; both the United States and the USSR cut funding with the 1991 negotiated peace settlement.

34. Jeffrey Record, *Beating Goliath: Why Insurgencies Win* (Washington, DC: Potomac Books, Inc., 2007), xi.

35. Data obtained from the UCDP/PRIO Armed Conflict Data Set, version v4–2009, http://www.prio.no/CSCW/Datasets/Armed-Conflict/UCDP-PRIO/.

36. "China Overtakes Japan as World's Second-Biggest Economy," *Bloomberg News*, 16 Aug 2010, http://www.bloomberg.com/news/2010-08-16/china-economy-passes-japan-s-in-second-quarter-capping-three-decade-rise.html.

37. Jonathan Pollack "American Perceptions of Chinese Military Power" in *The China Threat: Perceptions, Myths and Reality*, eds. Herbert Yee and Ian Storey (New York, NY: RoutledgeCurzon, 2002), 44, outlines an array of Chinese military advances.

38. Aaron Friedberg, "Implications of the Financial Crisis for the US-China Rivalry," *Survival: Global Politics and Strategy* 52, no. 4, August–September 2010, 33–36, describes a wide range of effects resulting from the financial crisis on US–Chinese rivalries.

39. Jack S. Levy, "Power Transition Theory and the Rise of China," in *China's Ascent: Power, Security and the Future of International Politics*, eds. Robert S. Ross and Zhu Feng (Ithaca, NY: Cornell University Press, 2008), 32, argues China will challenge the US in Asia and to a lesser extent Africa only, until it develops sufficient power projection capability to expand further. Zhu Feng "China's Rise will be Peaceful: Unipolarity Matters," in *China's Ascent: Power, Security and the Future of International Politics*, eds. Robert S. Ross and Zhu Feng (Ithaca, NY: Cornell University Press, 2008), 53, claims China's rise will be peaceful, using soft balancing against the United States in a unipolar construct.

40. John Ikenberry, "The Rise of China: Power, Institutions and the Western Order," in *China's Ascent: Power, Security and the Future of International Politics*, eds. Robert S. Ross and Zhu Feng (Ithaca, NY: Cornell University Press, 2008), 92, shows how strengthening international institutions will force China to peaceably rise within them,

rather than mounting a challenge to the international order. Jonathan Kirschner, in *China's Ascent: Power, Security and the Future of International Politics*, eds. Robert S. Ross and Zhu Feng (Ithaca, NY: Cornell University Press, 2008), 239, claims that while Sino–US economic tensions will sometimes be high, war is also unlikely over this issue.

41. Robert Kaplan, "The Geography of Chinese Power: How Far can Beijing Reach on Land and at Sea?" *Foreign Affairs* 89, no. 3, May/June 2010, 2, states that such actions are also conflictual in that they are shifting the balance of power in the Eastern Hemisphere, which ". . .must mightily concern the United States."

42. Jacqueline Newmyer, "Oil, Arms and Influence: The Indirect Strategy behind Chinese Military Modernization," *Orbis* 53, no. 2, February 2009, 207, also shows how Chinese military modernization will soon make US efforts to protect Taiwan too costly to consider, and obviate the need for a Chinese use of force in such a conflict.

43. Andrew Scobell, *China's Use of Military Force: Beyond the Great Wall and the Long March* (New York, NY: Cambridge University Press, 2003), 189-91, describes Chinese offensive capabilities during this incident.

44. David Kang, *China Rising: Peace, Power and Order in East Asia* (New York, NY: Columbia University Press, 2007), 197–98, makes a strong case that regional balancing against China is thus unlikely.

45. Robert Norris and Hans Kristensen, "Chinese Nuclear Forces, 2010," *Bulletin of the Atomic Scientists* 66, no. 6 (November 2010): 134.

46. Aaron Friedberg, "The Future of U.S.–China Relations: Is Conflict Inevitable?" *International Security* 30, no. 2 (Fall 2005): 17–19, argues that the costs of such conflict will cause both sides to carefully avoid direct conflict.

47. Kaplan, "The Geography of Chinese Power," 2, argues China is anxious to secure energy, metals and strategic minerals to meet these needs.

48. Friedberg, "The Future of U.S.–China Relations," 17–19, also highlights China's potential for economic growth and its implications.

49. Kaplan, "The Geography of Chinese Power," 4, notes that resource acquisition is "the primary goal of China's foreign policy everywhere."

50. Grecia Matos and Lorie Wagner, "Consumption of Materials in the United States, 1900–1995," *Annual Review of Energy and Environment*, 23–107, http://pubs.usgs.gov/annrev/ar-23-107/aerdocnew.pdf, 4.

51. Data obtained from the US–China Economic and Security Review Commission, "2010 Report to Congress," http://www.uscc.gov/annual_report/2010/10report_chapters.php, 183.

52. Friedberg, "The Future of U.S.–China Relations," 19, shows how rising power states such as China will take necessary steps to

ensure its access to required resources; he also states that disputes over these issues are "seldom resolved peacefully."

53. These states are Libya, Nigeria, Angola, Algeria, Egypt, Sudan, and the Democratic Republic of the Congo. Reserve information was obtained from *CIA: The World Fact Book*, https://www.cia.gov/library/publications/the-world-factbook/.

54. "China to Help South Africa Develop Mineral Wealth," *Bloomberg News*, 25 August 2010.

55. Peter Lewis, "China in Africa," *The Bretton Woods Committee* 2, no. 1 (Spring 2007): 1.

56. Bill Emmott, *Rivals: How the Power Struggle between China, India and Japan will Shape our Next Decade* (Orlando, FL: Mariner Books, 2009), 53.

57. Jonathan Holslag and Sara Van Hoeymissen, *The Limits of Socialization: The Search for EU-China Cooperation towards Security Challenges in Africa*, Policy Report (Brussels, Belgium: Brussels Institute of Contemporary China Studies, 30 May 2010). China currently imports more than a quarter of its oil from Africa.

58. Economic data from Lewis, "China in Africa," 12.

59. Stephen Burgess, "Sustainability of Strategic Minerals in Southern Africa and Potential Conflicts and Partnerships," Air War College Research Paper, 2010, http://www.usafa.edu/df/inss/Research%20Papers/2010/Report%20B

urgess%20Southern%20Africa%20Strategic%20Minerals.pdf, 4. Burgess argues that the US has traditionally relied on free market forces in Africa and elsewhere for access to its strategic resource needs. However, China's monopolistic practices in Africa mean that future access to these materials is no longer guaranteed and may be in serious jeopardy.

60. Note for example Tunisia's recent ouster of President Ali and the recent antigovernment rebellion in Egypt.

61. Steven R. David, *Catastrophic Consequences: Civil Wars and American Interests* (Baltimore, MD: Johns Hopkins University Press, 2008), describes how such regimes provide fertile ground for civil wars.

62. Burgess, "Sustainability of Strategic Minerals," describes the US need for "defense critical materials," primarily available only from Africa, which the United States must have access to in order to maintain its national security. These include platinum, cobalt, chromium, and manganese—each is vital to US defense and civilian industrial sectors and found primarily in African states and Russia. The lack of these materials would represent a critical loss in US ability to manufacture weapons and other defense systems and thus conceivably weaken US national security.

63. Barack H. Obama, *National Security Strategy* (Washington DC: Government Printing Office, May 2010), 6.

64. Examples include the F-35 Joint Strike Fighter, *Virginia*-class submarines, and ballistic missile defense programs.

65. Andrew F. Krepinevich, Jr., "The Pentagon's Wasting Assets: The Eroding Foundations of American Power" *Foreign Affairs* 88, no. 4 (July/August 2009): 28–33. Such "wasting assets" have implications for future US foreign policy as well, as outlined in Donna M. Oglesby, "Statecraft at the Crossroads: A New Diplomacy," *SAIS Review* 29, no. 2 (Summer/Fall 2009): 94.

www.ingramcontent.com/pod-product-compliance
Lightning Source LLC
Chambersburg PA
CBHW081804280526
45789CB00008B/2993